CONTENTS

PASSION INTO RICHES

The Ultimate Guide of YouTube Mastery - The Legacy Edition

* * *

"Passion is energy. Feel the power that comes from focusing on what excites you."

- OPRAH WINFREY

This book is dedicated to all the dreamers, doers, and creators out there who are passionate about turning their passions into successful careers. May the insights and strategies in this book inspire and empower you to unlock your true potential and achieve your dreams.

I want to help you turn your passion into riches, and I hope this book provides you with valuable insights, tips, and strategies to achieve your goals. Remember, success is not just about making money but also about finding fulfillment and making a positive impact in the world. So, whether you're an aspiring YouTuber or an entrepreneur looking to monetize your passion, I believe this book can help you on your journey.

Finally, I want to express my gratitude to all those who have supported and encouraged me throughout this journey. To my family and friends, thank you for always believing in me and for being my constant source of inspiration. And to my subscribers and viewers, thank you for giving me the opportunity to share my passion with you and for being a part of my success. This book is dedicated to all of you.

INTRODUCTION

OVERVIEW OF THE BOOK

The book's topic is focused on making money on YouTube, and its purpose is to provide readers with a comprehensive guide to building and monetizing a successful YouTube channel. YouTube has become a powerful platform for content creators to build their audience, monetize their content, and earn a living doing what they love. However, achieving success on YouTube requires a deep understanding of the platform, its users, and the strategies that can be used to effectively build an audience and generate revenue.

This book aims to provide readers with a detailed overview of the strategies and tactics used by successful YouTubers, as well as practical advice on creating high-quality content, engaging with your audience, and building a business around your YouTube channel. Whether you are just starting out on YouTube or looking to take your channel to the next level, this book will provide you with the knowledge and tools needed to succeed in the competitive world of YouTube content creation and monetization.

IMPORTANCE OF YOUTUBE AS A PLATFORM FOR MAKING MONEY

YouTube has become an incredibly important platform for making money due to its massive user base and the various monetization opportunities it offers to content creators. With over 2 billion monthly active users and over 1 billion hours of video watched every day, YouTube provides content creators with a vast audience to reach and engage with.

One of the most popular ways to make money on YouTube is through advertising revenue. YouTube offers it's content creators the ability to monetize their videos through ads that are displayed before, during, or after their videos. Creators earn a share of the revenue generated by these ads based on factors such as video views, ad clicks, and ad impressions. Successful YouTubers can earn significant amounts of money through advertising revenue alone.

In addition to advertising revenue, there are many other ways to monetize a YouTube channel, such as sponsored content, merchandise sales, and fan funding.

YouTube also offers it's content creators the ability to join the YouTube Partner Program, which provides additional monetization options and access to exclusive features.

Overall, YouTube's massive user base and various monetization opportunities make it a highly attractive platform for anyone looking to make money through online content creation. As such, Content creators need to understand the various strategies and tactics needed to effectively build and monetize a successful YouTube channel.

UNDERSTANDING YOUTUBE AND ITS POTENTIAL

OVERVIEW OF YOUTUBE AS A PLATFORM FOR MAKING MONEY

YouTube has become a major platform for content creators to make money online. With over 2 billion monthly active users and over 1 billion hours of video watched every day, YouTube provides a vast audience for creators to reach and engage with.

One of the most popular ways for content creators to make money on YouTube is through advertising revenue. YouTube offers to its content creators the ability to monetize their videos through ads that are displayed before, during, or after their videos. Creators earn a share of the revenue generated by these ads based on factors such as video views, ad clicks, and ad impressions. Successful YouTubers can earn significant amounts of money through advertising revenue alone.

In addition to advertising revenue, there are many other ways to monetize a YouTube channel. One of the most popular is sponsored content, where creators partner with brands to promote products or services in their videos. Another way to make money on YouTube is through fan funding, where viewers can donate money to support their favorite creators.

To be successful on YouTube, content creators need to build a loyal and engaged audience. This requires creating high-quality content that is optimized for search and discovery, as well as engaging with viewers through social media and other channels. Successful YouTubers also need to be strategic in how they monetize their content, by diversifying their revenue streams and partnering with brands and other creators to expand their reach.

Overall, YouTube provides content creators with a powerful platform to reach a massive audience and generate income through various monetization strategies. As such, it has become an essential tool for anyone looking to make money through online content creation.

BENEFITS AND DRAWBACKS OF USING YOUTUBE TO MAKE MONEY

Using YouTube to make money offers a range of benefits and drawbacks that content creators should consider before starting a channel. Here are some of the key benefits and drawbacks.

The Benefits of YouTube include:
- Large Audience
- Low barriers to entry
- Diverse monetization options
- Flexibility
- Long-term income potential
- Opportunity for creative expression
- Analytics tools
- Career Development

The Drawbacks are:
- Competition
- Changing algorithms
- High production costs
- Time-consuming
- Uncertain income
- Cyber Harassment

Large Audience

Having a large audience is beneficial for several reasons. First, it provides content creators with a vast pool of potential viewers who can engage with their content, share it with others, and help grow their audience. Additionally, a large audience increases the likelihood of generating income from various monetization methods, such as advertising revenue, sponsorships, merchandise sales, and fan funding.

For businesses and brands, having a large audience on YouTube can also be advantageous. It can help them reach potential customers and build brand awareness on a platform where people spend a significant amount of time-consuming video content. Brands can also leverage the audience insights provided by YouTube to create targeted ad campaigns and track the performance of their videos.

In summary, having a large audience on YouTube can be a significant advantage for content creators and brands alike. It provides a massive potential viewership and opens up opportunities for monetization and brand building. However, building and maintaining a large audience on YouTube requires time, effort, and a well-planned content strategy.

Low Barriers to Entry

YouTube has low barriers to entry, which means that anyone can create an account and start uploading content to the platform. Unlike traditional media industries like TV or film, YouTube does not require creators to have professional training, equipment, or connections to get started.

This low barrier to entry has several advantages for content creators. First, it allows them to showcase their talents and skills without the need for significant investment in production equipment or a distribution network. This means that even creators with limited resources can potentially reach a vast audience on YouTube.

As creators can test and refine their content without fear of financial or reputational loss, This encourages a diverse range of content on the platform, with creators experimenting with new formats, styles, and genres.

Finally, low barriers to entry create opportunities for creators to build their brand and reputation from scratch, without needing to rely on established media networks or production studios.

However, the low barriers to entry on YouTube can also create some challenges. With so many creators vying for attention, it can be challenging to stand out and attract an audience. Additionally, the lack of formal training or professional guidance can lead to issues with quality control or ethical standards. Nonetheless, overall, the low barriers to entry on YouTube create a more accessible and democratized media landscape, offering opportunities for creators who may not have had them otherwise.

Diverse Monetization Options

YouTube offers content creators a diverse range of monetization options, which allows them to earn money from their content in various ways.
These include:

- Advertising revenue: YouTube's Partner Program allows creators to earn a share of the advertising revenue generated from ads displayed on their videos.
- Sponsorships and brand deals: Creators can work with brands or other companies to promote their products or services in their videos, earning money in exchange for their promotion.
- Merchandise sales: YouTube creators can sell merchandise related to their channel, such as t-shirts, mugs, or other products with their branding or logos.
- Fan funding: YouTube's Super Chat and Super Stickers features allow viewers to donate money to their favourite creators during livestreams or other content.
- Channel memberships: Creators can offer their viewers the option to become channel members, which grants access to exclusive content or other benefits in exchange for a monthly fee.
- Licensing: YouTube creators can license their content for use in other media, such as TV shows, films, or advertisements, in exchange for a licensing fee.

These diverse monetization options are beneficial for creators because they provide multiple streams of income and allow them to choose the methods that work best for their content and audience. This flexibility can also help creators diversify their revenue and protect against changes in advertising rates or other external factors that may affect their income.

Flexibility

Flexibility is a key advantage of using YouTube as a platform for making money. The platform offers creators the flexibility to create and upload content on their own schedule, as well as choose from a range of monetization options to suit their needs.

For example, creators can choose to monetize their content through advertising revenue, sponsorships, merchandise sales, fan funding, channel memberships, or licensing. This range of options allows creators to choose the methods that work best for their content and audience, as well as diversify their revenue streams and protect against changes in advertising rates or other external factors.

Additionally, YouTube allows creators to choose the type of content they want to create, whether it's vlogs, tutorials, reviews, or other formats. This flexibility means that creators can experiment with different content types and refine their skills over time, as well as cater to their audience's interests and preferences.

Another aspect of flexibility on YouTube is the ability to engage with the audience. Creators can respond to comments, host live streams, and engage with viewers in other ways, which can help build a loyal audience and foster a sense of community around their content.

Overall, the flexibility of YouTube as a platform for making money offers creators the ability to create and monetize content on their own terms. This flexibility can be particularly beneficial for those who may have other commitments, such as a full-time job or family responsibilities, as it allows them to create content and earn money on a schedule that works for them.

Long-Term Income Potential

One of the benefits of using YouTube as a platform for making money is the long-term income potential it offers. Unlike some other forms of income, such as a traditional job where earnings are tied to the number of hours worked, creating and monetizing content on YouTube can generate income over an extended period of time. Here are a few reasons why YouTube has long-term income potential:

- Evergreen content: YouTube videos can continue to generate income long after they are uploaded. This is because many types of content, such as tutorials or product reviews, are evergreen and can continue to be relevant and useful to viewers over time.

- Passive income: Once a YouTube video is uploaded and monetized, it can continue to earn money passively over time. This means that even if a creator takes a break from creating new content, their existing videos can continue to generate income.

- Increased audience and revenue over time: As a creator's channel grows and gains more subscribers and views, their potential revenue also increases. This means that creators can earn more money over time as their audience and influence grows.

- Multiple streams of income: As mentioned earlier, YouTube offers multiple ways to monetize content, from advertising revenue to sponsorships, merchandise sales, fan funding, channel memberships, and licensing. This diversification of revenue streams can help creators earn a stable income over the long term.

In summary, YouTube offers long-term income potential for creators through evergreen content, passive income, increased audience and revenue over time, and diversification of revenue streams. This makes it an attractive option for those who are interested in creating content and earning a sustainable income over an extended period of time.

Opportunity For Creative Expression

One of the benefits of using YouTube as a platform for making money is the opportunity for creative expression that it offers. YouTube allows creators to showcase their unique perspectives and talents through video content, and offers a platform for them to reach a global audience.

Here are a few reasons why YouTube offers an opportunity for creative expression:

- No gatekeepers: Unlike traditional media outlets, YouTube allows anyone to create and upload content without the need for approval from gatekeepers such as publishers or production companies. This means that creators have the freedom to create content on their own terms and express themselves in their own unique way.

- Niche content: YouTube allows creators to create content that caters to specific niches and interests, which can be difficult to do through traditional media outlets. This means that creators can express themselves through content that truly reflects their interests and passions.

- Visual storytelling: Video is a powerful medium for visual storytelling, and YouTube offers a platform for creators to tell their stories through video content. This allows creators to use their creativity to craft compelling narratives and engage with their audience in a unique way.

- Community building: YouTube allows creators to build a community of followers who appreciate their content and share their interests. This means that creators can connect with their audience and receive feedback and support for their creative efforts.

In summary, YouTube offers an opportunity for creative expression through its lack of gatekeepers, ability to cater to niche content, powerful visual storytelling capabilities, and community-building features. This makes it an attractive option for creators who want to express themselves creatively and reach a global audience with their unique perspectives and talents.

Analytics Tools

One of the benefits of using YouTube as a platform for making money is the availability of analytics tools that allow creators to track the performance of their content and make data-driven decisions to optimize their revenue streams. YouTube's analytics tools offer valuable insights into a variety of metrics related to a creator's channel and individual videos.

Here are a few ways that YouTube's analytics tools can be useful for creators:

- Audience insights: YouTube's analytics tools provide information about a creator's audience, including demographics such as age, gender, and location. This information can help creators tailor their content to better serve their audience and make data-driven decisions about their marketing efforts.

- Video performance: YouTube's analytics tools offer detailed information about how each video is performing, including views, watch time, engagement metrics, and more. This information can help creators identify which videos are resonating with their audience and make decisions about which types of content to create in the future.

- Revenue metrics: YouTube's analytics tools provide information about how much money a creator is earning from their content, including ad revenue, sponsorships, and other monetization methods. This information can help creators make decisions about how to optimize their revenue streams and improve their overall earnings.

- Channel performance: YouTube's analytics tools offer insights into overall channel performance, including subscriber growth, audience retention, and more. This information can help creators identify areas for improvement and make data-driven decisions about how to grow their channel and audience.

In summary, YouTube's analytics tools provide valuable insights into a variety of metrics related to a creator's channel and content performance. These insights can help creators make data-driven decisions to optimize their revenue streams and grow their audience over time.

Career Development

Using YouTube as a platform for making money can offer significant opportunities for career development. YouTube creators can leverage their success on the platform to pursue a variety of other career opportunities and build their personal brand.

Here are a few ways that YouTube can support career development:

- Brand building: By creating a strong personal brand on YouTube, creators can establish themselves as experts in their field and build a loyal following of fans. This can lead to opportunities for brand partnerships, sponsorships, and other collaborations that can help to further build their personal brand and expand their reach.

- Career opportunities: Successful YouTube creators can use their platform to pursue a variety of other career opportunities, such as speaking engagements, book deals, and other media appearances. This can help to establish them as thought leaders in their industry and open up new career paths.

- Skill development: Creating content on YouTube requires a variety of skills, such as video production, storytelling, and audience engagement. As creators develop these skills over time, they can use them to pursue other career opportunities in related fields, such as media production, marketing, or public speaking.

- Entrepreneurship: Many successful YouTube creators have gone on to start their own businesses or pursue other entrepreneurial ventures. By leveraging their personal brand and audience on YouTube, creators can build a following that can support their new ventures and help them achieve success in other areas.

In summary, YouTube can offer significant opportunities for career development by providing a platform for personal brand building, creating opportunities for career advancement, and helping creators develop valuable skills and entrepreneurial ventures.

Competition

Competition is a significant factor in the world of YouTube as it is a platform with millions of content creators. With such a large number of creators vying for views, subscribers, and advertising dollars, it can be challenging for newcomers to break into the scene and establish themselves.

Here are a few things to consider regarding competition on YouTube:

- Saturation: One of the biggest challenges facing new creators is the saturation of the platform. With millions of videos uploaded every day, it can be difficult to stand out and attract an audience.
- Niche focus: Successful creators often find success by focusing on a specific niche or topic area. This allows them to differentiate themselves from the competition and establish themselves as experts in their field.
- Quality content: In a crowded field, quality content is more important than ever. Creators need to create content that is unique, engaging, and adds value to their audience in order to stand out and attract viewers.
- Algorithmic changes: YouTube's algorithm is constantly evolving, which can make it difficult for creators to keep up with changes and stay relevant. Creators need to stay informed about changes to the algorithm and adjust their content strategies accordingly.
- Collaboration: Collaboration with other creators can help to increase exposure and reach a wider audience. Successful creators often work together to create content that appeals to both of their audiences, which can help to increase their viewership and build their following. As Teamwork leads to Dreamwork, Collaboration is one of the best method to reach a wide Audience.

In summary, competition is a significant factor in the world of YouTube, and creators need to find ways to differentiate themselves from the competition in order to stand out and attract an audience. By focusing on a niche, creating high-quality content, staying informed about algorithmic changes, and collaborating with other creators, creators can increase their chances of success on the platform.

Changing Algorithms

YouTube's algorithm is constantly evolving, which means that creators need to stay informed about changes and adjust their content strategies accordingly. The algorithm determines which videos are recommended to viewers, and it takes into account a variety of factors, such as watch time, engagement, and video quality.

Here are a few things to consider regarding changing algorithms on YouTube:

- Algorithm updates: YouTube regularly updates its algorithm to improve the user experience and provide more relevant content to viewers. Creators need to stay informed about these updates and adjust their content strategies accordingly.

- Watch time: One of the most important factors in the algorithm is watch time, which is the amount of time viewers spend watching a video. Creators need to create engaging content that keeps viewers watching in order to improve their chances of being recommended by the algorithm.

- Engagement: The algorithm also takes into account engagement factors, such as likes, comments, and shares. Creators need to encourage engagement by asking viewers to like, comment, and share their videos.

- Video quality: The algorithm also takes into account video quality, such as resolution, audio quality, and production value. Creators need to create high-quality videos that are visually appealing and easy to watch.

- Changes in viewer behaviour: The algorithm also changes based on viewer behaviour, such as the type of content they watch and the devices they use. Creators need to stay informed about these changes and adjust their content strategies accordingly.

In summary, YouTube's algorithm is constantly evolving, and creators need to stay informed about changes and adjust their content strategies accordingly. By focusing on watch time, engagement, video quality, and changes in viewer behaviour, creators can improve their chances of success on the platform.

High Production Costs

Producing high-quality videos for YouTube can be costly, and this can be a significant drawback for creators looking to make money on the platform.

Here are a few things to consider regarding high production costs on YouTube:

- Equipment costs: Producing high-quality videos requires high-quality equipment, which can be expensive. Cameras, lighting equipment, microphones, and editing software can all add up and be a significant investment for creators.
- Time costs: Producing high-quality videos also requires a significant time investment. Creators need to spend time researching, planning, filming, and editing their videos, which can take hours or even days.
- Outsourcing costs: Many creators outsource certain aspects of video production, such as editing or graphic design. However, outsourcing can be costly and eat into profits.
- Cost-benefit analysis: Creators need to weigh the benefits of producing high-quality videos against the costs. High-quality videos can attract more views and higher advertising rates, but if the costs are too high, it may not be worth it in the long run.
- Lower production options: There are ways to produce high-quality videos without breaking the bank. Creators can use affordable equipment, shoot in natural light, and learn basic editing skills to produce quality content on a budget.

In summary, producing high-quality videos for YouTube can be costly, but it can also be a worthwhile investment if it leads to more views and higher advertising rates. Creators need to weigh the benefits against the costs and find ways to produce quality content on a budget if necessary.

Time-Consuming

Creating content for YouTube can be a time-consuming process, and this can be a significant drawback for creators looking to make money on the platform.

Here are a few things to consider regarding the time-consuming nature of YouTube:

- Content creation: Creating quality content for YouTube takes time. Creators need to brainstorm ideas, research topics, write scripts, and film and edit videos. Depending on the type of content, this can take hours or even days to complete.
- Consistency: To build an audience on YouTube, creators need to be consistent in their content creation. This means producing videos on a regular schedule, which can be challenging and time-consuming.
- Community engagement: To build a community on YouTube, creators need to engage with their audience. This means responding to comments, creating content based on feedback, and participating in social media. This can be a time-consuming process but is important for building a loyal audience.
- Promotion: Promoting content on YouTube requires time and effort. Creators need to promote their videos through social media, email lists, and other platforms to reach a wider audience.
- Time management: Managing time is essential for successful YouTube creators. They need to balance content creation, promotion, and engagement with other responsibilities, such as work or school.

In summary, creating content for YouTube can be time-consuming, but it is an essential part of building a successful channel. Creators need to manage their time effectively, be consistent in their content creation, engage with their audience, and promote their content to reach a wider audience.

Uncertain Income

One of the main drawbacks of using YouTube to make money is the uncertain income it can provide due to the Contents we make.

Here are a few things to consider regarding the uncertainty of income on YouTube:

- Ad revenue fluctuations: One of the primary ways creators make money on YouTube is through ad revenue. However, the amount of money earned from ads can fluctuate depending on factors such as views, engagement, and ad rates.
- Changes to monetization policies: YouTube's monetization policies can change at any time, which can affect the income of creators. For example, changes to the eligibility requirements for monetization can impact smaller channels that rely on ad revenue.
- Sponsorship and brand deals: Many creators supplement their income with sponsorship and brand deals. However, these deals are not always consistent and can be affected by factors such as changes in the market, consumer behaviour, or the creator's audience.
- Lack of job security: Being a YouTube creator does not come with the same level of job security as a traditional job. Income can fluctuate and is not guaranteed, which can create uncertainty and financial instability.
- Diversification: To mitigate the risk of uncertain income, many creators diversify their revenue streams. This can include merchandise sales, affiliate marketing, or offering premium content to subscribers.

In summary, the uncertain income associated with YouTube can be a significant drawback for creators looking to make money on the platform. Changes to ad revenue, monetization policies, and sponsorship deals can all impact income, and there is no guarantee of job security. To mitigate the risk of uncertain income, many creators diversify their revenue streams and explore other ways to supplement their income.

Cyber Harassment

Cyber harassment on YouTube refers to any kind of abusive or harassing behaviour that is directed towards creators or viewers on the platform. This type of harassment can take many forms, including cyberbullying, hate speech, doxing, and threats of violence.

Cyber harassment can have a serious impact on individuals, causing emotional distress, anxiety, and even depression. In some cases, cyber harassment can lead to real-world harm, including physical violence.

Creators on YouTube are particularly vulnerable to cyber harassment, as they often put themselves in the public eye and are open to criticism and feedback from viewers. Cyber harassment can be especially harmful to young or inexperienced creators who may not have the emotional resilience to handle negative comments and feedback.

YouTube has community guidelines in place that prohibit hate speech, harassment, and other forms of abusive behaviour.

The platform also has reporting tools that allow creators and viewers to report abusive behaviour. YouTube has a team of reviewers who can review reports and take action against violators, including removing content and suspending or terminating accounts.

Despite YouTube's efforts to combat cyber harassment, it remains a significant issue on the platform. Creators and viewers should take steps to protect themselves, including reporting abusive behaviour, blocking users who engage in harassment, and seeking support from friends and family or mental health professionals.

Cyber harassment is a significant issue on YouTube, and it can affect creators of all ages. Children, in particular, can be vulnerable to cyber harassment on the platform.

Here's an overview of cyber harassment on YouTube and the steps the platform has taken to address it:

    I. Cyber harassment on YouTube: Cyber harassment on YouTube can take many forms, including cyberbullying, hate speech, and doxing. Creators can receive hateful comments, be targeted by trolls or bots, and even receive death threats.

    II. Impact on children: Children who create content on YouTube can be particularly vulnerable to cyber harassment. They may not have the same level of emotional maturity as adult creators and may be more susceptible to the negative effects of harassment.

    III. YouTube's response: YouTube has taken several steps to address cyber harassment on the platform. These include:

        A. Community guidelines: YouTube has community guidelines that prohibit hate speech, harassment, and other forms of abusive behaviour.

B. Reporting tools: Creators and viewers can report abusive behaviour through YouTube's reporting tools. YouTube has a team of reviewers that can review reports and take action against violators.

C. Age restrictions: YouTube has age restrictions for certain types of content, which can help protect children from exposure to inappropriate material.

D. Creator resources: YouTube provides resources to help creators deal with cyber harassment. This includes tips on how to handle abusive comments and how to report abusive behaviour.

IV. Additional steps: In 2019, YouTube announced new policies to protect children's privacy and safety on the platform. These include:

A. Limiting data collection: YouTube will limit the data it collects on children's content to comply with COPPA (Children's Online Privacy Protection Act).

B. Removing comments: YouTube will disable comments on videos featuring minors in certain situations to help protect children from cyber harassment.

C. Age-appropriate content: YouTube will introduce new features that will allow parents to restrict their children's access to age-inappropriate content.

In summary, cyber harassment is a significant issue on YouTube, and children can be particularly vulnerable to its negative effects. YouTube has taken steps to address cyber harassment on the platform, including community guidelines, reporting tools, age restrictions, and resources for creators. Additionally, the platform has introduced new policies to protect children's privacy and safety, including limiting data collection, removing comments, and providing age-appropriate content.

FINDING YOUR NICHE AND BUILDING YOUR BRAND

IDENTIFYING YOUR NICHE AND TARGET AUDIENCE (OVERVIEW)

Identifying your niche and target audience is a critical step in building a successful YouTube channel. Your niche is the area of focus for your channel, and it's important to choose a niche that you're passionate about and knowledgeable in. Your niche should also be specific enough to differentiate your channel from others but broad enough to attract a sizable audience.

Once you've identified your niche, the next step is to define your target audience. Your target audience is the group of people you want to reach with your content, and it's important to have a clear understanding of who they are. You can use demographics like age, gender, and location to help define your target audience, but it's also important to consider their interests, needs, and motivations.

When defining your target audience, it's helpful to create a viewer persona or avatar. This is a fictional representation of your ideal viewer, and it can help you create content that resonates with them. Your viewer persona should include details like their age, gender, occupation, interests, and pain points. You can use this information to create content that addresses their needs and interests, and to craft your marketing messages to attract their attention.

By identifying your niche and target audience, you can create content that resonates with your viewers and build a loyal fan base. It's important to continually evaluate your niche and target audience and make adjustments as needed to ensure that you're meeting their needs and staying relevant.

TIPS TO IDENTIFY YOUR NICHE AND TARGET AUDIENCE

The Tips to Identify your Niche and target Audience are:

- Consider your passions and interests: The best way to create content that resonates with your audience is to create content that you are passionate about. Think about your hobbies, interests, and expertise to find a niche that aligns with your passions.
- Research popular niches: Look at what other successful YouTubers in your niche are doing, and consider what sets you apart from them. It's important to find a balance between creating content that is unique and stands out in a crowded field.
- Define your target audience: Once you've identified your niche, think about who your target audience is. Consider their age, gender, interests, and demographics. Understanding your audience will help you create content that resonates with them.
- Create a content plan: Once you've identified your niche and target audience, create a content plan that aligns with your goals. Consider the types of content your audience is most likely to engage with, and create a schedule that works for you.
- Stay flexible: As you create content and build your audience, it's important to stay flexible and adjust your strategy as needed. Pay attention to your analytics and feedback from your audience, and be open to trying new things to keep your channel fresh and engaging.
- Test and refine your content: It's important to test different types of content and see what works best for your audience. Use your analytics to identify your most popular videos and refine your content strategy based on what is resonating with your viewers.
- Engage with your audience: Building a loyal fan base requires engagement and interaction with your audience. Respond to comments, ask for feedback, and create a community around your channel.
- Collaborate with other creators: Collaborating with other creators in your niche can help you reach new audiences and build relationships with other creators. Look for opportunities to collaborate on videos, podcasts, or other content.
- Stay up to date with trends: Keeping up with the latest trends and developments in your niche can help you create content that is relevant and engaging. Follow other creators, read industry blogs, and attend conferences or events to stay informed.
- Be authentic: Ultimately, the key to building a successful YouTube channel is to be authentic and true to yourself. Don't try to be someone you're not or create content that doesn't align with your values or interests. Your audience will

appreciate your authenticity and passion, and that will help you build a loyal fan base.

- Creating a brand identity for your YouTube channel is a critical step in establishing a strong online presence and standing out from the competition. Your brand identity is the image or personality that you want to convey to your audience, and it should reflect your niche, values, and unique selling proposition.
- To create a brand identity for your YouTube channel, start by choosing a name that's memorable, easy to spell, and relevant to your niche. Your name should also be available as a domain name and across social media platforms. Once you've chosen a name, create a logo that represents your channel and is consistent with your niche and target audience.
- Next, develop a consistent visual style for your channel. This includes choosing a color palette, fonts, and graphics that reflect your brand identity. Use these elements consistently across all of your videos, thumbnails, and social media profiles to create a cohesive brand image.
- In addition to visual elements, your brand identity should also include your tone of voice, messaging, and values. Determine the tone you want to use in your videos, such as informative, entertaining, or authoritative. Develop a messaging strategy that communicates your unique selling proposition and the benefits of watching your videos. Finally, define your values and use them to guide your content creation and engagement with your audience.
- By creating a strong brand identity for your YouTube channel, you can establish a recognizable and trustworthy online presence and build a loyal fan base. It's important to continually evaluate your brand identity and make adjustments as needed to ensure that it's relevant and resonates with your audience.
- A logo is a visual representation of your brand identity and is one of the most important elements of your branding strategy. It's the first thing that viewers see when they come across your channel, and it should immediately communicate your niche, values, and personality.
- When designing a logo for your YouTube channel, consider your niche and target audience. Your logo should be relevant to your niche and appeal to your target audience. For example, if you create videos about fitness, your logo could include a fitness-related symbol, such as a dumbbell or a running shoe.
- It's also important to choose a logo design that is visually appealing and easy to recognize. A simple and memorable design is often more effective than a complex or cluttered one. Make sure your logo is easy to read and

stands out from the background.

- Finally, use your logo consistently across all of your branding materials, including your YouTube channel, social media profiles, and website. This will help to establish brand recognition and make it easier for viewers to find and remember your channel.
- Overall, a logo is an essential component of creating a strong brand identity for your YouTube channel. It's important to invest time and resources into designing a logo that effectively represents your brand and appeals to your target audience.

Here is a Story about a Lady named Sarah, who showed her Passion for Cooking on YouTube and made a living out of it.

Once there was a young woman named Sarah who loved baking. She would often spend her free time experimenting with new recipes and decorating beautiful cakes and pastries. One day, while scrolling through YouTube, she stumbled upon a baking channel with thousands of subscribers. She realized that there was an opportunity to turn her passion into a successful YouTube channel.

Excited by the idea, Sarah started to think about what made her unique. She decided to focus on vegan baking, as she was passionate about creating delicious treats without the use of animal products. She spent hours researching vegan baking techniques and perfecting her recipes.

After a few months of hard work, Sarah launched her channel, "Vegan Baking with Sarah." She started with just a few subscribers, but she remained consistent in her content creation and engaged with her audience regularly. She also utilized social media to promote her videos and engage with her viewers.

Over time, Sarah's channel grew in popularity, and she became known as an expert in vegan baking. She was able to monetize her channel through sponsorships and merchandise, and she even wrote a cookbook that became a bestseller. Sarah's passion for vegan baking not only allowed her to turn her hobby into a successful business but also helped her to make a positive impact by spreading awareness about animal rights and sustainable living.

Sarah's story is a testament to the power of identifying your niche and turning your passion into a successful business. By focusing on what made her unique and staying true to her values, she was able to build a loyal following and create a fulfilling career doing something she loved.

DEVELOPING A CONTENT STRATEGY AND EDITORIAL CALENDAR

Developing a content strategy and editorial calendar is crucial for the success of your YouTube channel. It helps you plan and organize your content, so you can consistently create and publish high-quality videos that resonate with your target audience.

To develop a content strategy, start by defining your niche and identifying the topics that your target audience is interested in. This will help you create content that is relevant and valuable to your viewers.

Next, consider the format and style of your videos. Will they be instructional, entertaining, or a mix of both? Will they be short or long-form? Will you use animations, music, or special effects? Answering these questions will help you create a consistent style and tone for your videos.

Once you have a clear understanding of your content strategy, it's time to create an editorial calendar. This is a schedule that outlines when you will publish each video and what topics they will cover. It helps you stay organized and ensures that you are consistently creating and publishing content.

When creating your editorial calendar, consider important events or holidays that may be relevant to your niche. This will help you create timely and relevant content that is more likely to resonate with your audience.

Overall, developing a content strategy and editorial calendar is essential for the success of your YouTube channel. It helps you create and publish high-quality content that is relevant to your target audience, and ensures that you are consistently delivering value to your viewers.

CREATING ENGAGING AND MARKETABLE CONTENT

CREATING HIGH-QUALITY VIDEO CONTENT

Creating high-quality video content is essential for the success of your YouTube channel. The quality of your videos will determine how engaging and valuable they are to your audience, which in turn affects your views, engagement, and overall success on the platform.

To create high-quality video content, start by investing in a good camera and microphone. The camera should be capable of shooting in at least 1080p HD resolution, and the microphone should be able to capture clear and crisp audio.

Next, pay attention to lighting and composition. Proper lighting can greatly enhance the visual quality of your videos, while good composition can make your videos look more professional and engaging.

When it comes to content, make sure to deliver value to your viewers. Consider the topics and themes that are relevant to your niche and target audience, and create content that is informative, entertaining, or both.

In addition to the content itself, pay attention to the editing and post-production process. This includes trimming footage, adding transitions, and including music or other sound effects. Good editing can greatly enhance the visual and auditory quality of your videos, making them more engaging and valuable to your audience.

Finally, don't forget to optimize your videos for YouTube. This includes using relevant keywords in your titles and descriptions, adding tags to your videos, and creating eye-catching thumbnails that entice viewers to click on your videos.

Overall, creating high-quality video content is essential for the success of your YouTube channel. By investing in good equipment, paying attention to lighting and composition, delivering valuable content, and optimizing your videos for YouTube, you can create engaging and valuable content that resonates with your audience and helps you grow your channel.

OPTIMIZE YOUR VIDEOS FOR SEARCH

SEO also known as Search Engine Optimization is the practice of optimizing content in a way that makes it more visible and discoverable by search engines. In the context of YouTube, this means optimizing your videos for search to increase their visibility and reach on the platform.

Optimizing your videos for search begins with understanding how YouTube's search algorithm works. The algorithm takes into account various factors such as the video's title, description, tags, and engagement metrics (such as views, likes, and comments) to determine the relevance and quality of the content. To optimize your videos for search, start by conducting keyword research to identify relevant and popular search terms related to your niche and target audience. Use these keywords in your video titles, descriptions, and tags to increase their relevance and visibility in search results.

Additionally, pay attention to engagement metrics such as views, likes, and comments, as these factors also influence your videos' visibility and ranking in search results. Encourage your viewers to engage with your videos by including calls-to-action in your content, such as asking them to like, comment, or subscribe to your channel. Another important aspect of optimizing your videos for search is creating high-quality and relevant content. YouTube's algorithm prioritizes content that is valuable and engaging to viewers, so make sure to deliver content that resonates with your audience and provides value.

Finally, don't forget about the importance of your video's thumbnail. A compelling and eye-catching thumbnail can greatly increase your videos' click-through rate and overall visibility in search results. Make sure to use high-quality and relevant images that accurately represent your video's content.

In summary, optimizing your videos for search is an important aspect of building a successful YouTube channel. By conducting keyword research, including relevant keywords in your video's metadata, focusing on engagement metrics, creating high-quality content, and using compelling thumbnails, you can increase your videos' visibility and reach on the platform.

CREATING CLICKABLE THUMBNAILS AND TITLES

Creating clickable thumbnails and titles is crucial for getting views and clicks on your videos. Thumbnails and titles are the first things people see when they come across your video in search results, suggested videos, or on your channel page. They need to be eye-catching and intriguing enough to make people want to click and watch.

When creating your thumbnail, use high-quality images that are relevant to your video's topic. Choose an image that is visually appealing and stands out from the rest. Use text overlay to provide additional context about the video's content or add a sense of urgency to encourage viewers to watch.

Your title should also be attention-grabbing and accurately reflect the video's content. Use keywords that people are likely to search for to help your video rank higher in search results. Keep it concise and to the point, while still conveying the value of your video.

Remember to avoid clickbait titles and thumbnails that are misleading or irrelevant to the video's content. While they may get you more clicks in the short term, they can harm your channel's reputation.

TIPS FOR CREATING CLICKABLE THUMBNAILS AND TITLES

BUILDING AND ENGAGING YOUR AUDIENCE

STRATEGIES FOR BUILDING YOUR AUDIENCE ON YOUTUBE

Building your audience on YouTube is an essential aspect of creating a successful channel. It refers to the process of attracting and retaining subscribers, viewers, and followers to your channel. The more viewers you have, the greater the opportunity to increase your engagement rate and monetize your channel effectively.

One of the most important strategies for building your audience is to create consistent and high-quality content that resonates with your target audience. Consistency means that you upload content on a regular schedule so that your audience knows when to expect new videos. High-quality content means that your videos are well-produced, visually appealing, and provide value to your viewers.

Another key strategy is to engage with your audience through comments, social media, and other channels. Responding to comments and messages, asking for feedback, and creating a community around your channel can help build loyalty and increase engagement.

Collaborating with other YouTubers in your niche can also be a great way to build your audience. By working with other creators, you can reach new viewers and potentially attract their subscribers to your channel.

Promoting your channel through social media and other channels can also help you build your audience. Sharing your videos on platforms like Instagram, Twitter, and Facebook can attract new viewers and potentially drive more traffic to your channel.

Lastly, leveraging YouTube's own tools, such as YouTube ads and YouTube search optimization, can also help you build your audience. YouTube ads can help you reach new viewers while optimizing your videos for search can increase the visibility of your channel to potential viewers searching for content in your niche.

In summary, building your audience on YouTube is important because it helps you increase your engagement rate, attract potential sponsors, and monetize your channel.

STRATEGY THAT COULD BUILD YOUR COMMUNITY

- Consistency: One of the most important factors in building your audience is consistency. You need to consistently create and upload content that your viewers will enjoy.
- Engagement: Engage with your viewers by responding to comments, asking for feedback, and running polls or contests. This helps to create a community around your channel and encourages viewers to keep coming back.
- Promotion: Promote your channel on social media platforms and collaborate with other YouTubers in your niche. This helps to increase your reach and exposure to potential viewers.
- SEO: Optimize your videos for search by including relevant keywords in your titles, descriptions, and tags. This helps your videos appear in search results and reach new viewers.
- Analytics: Use YouTube analytics to track your progress and understand what's working and what's not. This helps you make informed decisions about your content and strategy.
- Call-to-action: Include a call-to-action in your videos, such as asking viewers to subscribe or share your content. This helps to increase engagement and build your audience.
- Value: Provide value to your viewers by creating content that is informative, entertaining, or helpful. This helps to establish you as an authority in your niche and builds trust with your audience.

ENGAGING YOUR AUDIENCE VIA COMMUNITY BUILDING, SOCIAL MEDIA, AND MORE

Engaging your audience is an essential part of building a successful YouTube channel. Community building, social media, and other channels can help you connect with your viewers, build a relationship with them, and keep them engaged with your content.

One effective strategy for community building is to create a discussion forum or group for your viewers. This forum can be a place where you and your viewers can interact with each other, share ideas, and discuss your content. By encouraging your viewers to participate in the discussion, you can build a strong sense of community around your channel.

Social media can also be a powerful tool for engaging your audience. By creating social media accounts for your channel and sharing your videos on those platforms, you can reach a wider audience and attract new viewers to your channel. You can also use social media to interact with your viewers, respond to their comments and messages, and share behind-the-scenes content and updates.

In addition to community building and social media, there are other channels you can use to engage your audience. For example, you can create a blog or website that features your videos, post your videos on other video-sharing platforms, or collaborate with other YouTubers in your niche. The key is to find the channels that work best for your audience and your content and use them to build a strong and engaged following.

TIPS FOR ENGAGING YOUR AUDIENCE

- Interact with your audience: Respond to comments and messages, and create a sense of community by engaging with your viewers.
- Collaborate with other creators: Collaborating with other YouTubers can help you reach a wider audience and establish yourself as a member of the YouTube community.
- Use social media to promote your channel: Share your videos on social media platforms such as Twitter, Facebook, and Instagram to attract new viewers and promote your brand.
- Create a mailing list: Encourage your viewers to sign up for a mailing list so that you can keep in touch with them and let them know when you have new content available.
- Offer exclusive content: Provide your most loyal fans with exclusive content, such as behind-the-scenes footage, special giveaways, or sneak previews of upcoming videos.
- Host Q&A sessions: Host live Q&A sessions to give your viewers the opportunity to interact with you in real time and ask questions about your content.
- Attend industry events: Attend industry events, such as conventions and conferences, to network with other creators and learn more about the latest trends and best practices in the YouTube community.

By engaging your audience through community building, social media, and other channels, you can build a loyal following of viewers who are passionate about your content and eager to support your channel.

MONETIZE THROUGH AUDIENCE

Once you have built a loyal audience, you can start monetizing your channel through various revenue streams.

Some of the most popular ways to monetize your audience on YouTube include:

- Sponsorships: You can partner with brands to create sponsored content on your channel. These partnerships can generate significant revenue, but it's important to make sure the brand aligns with your values and interests.
- Merchandise: Many YouTubers sell their own merchandise, such as T-shirts, hats, and other branded items. This is a great way to engage with your audience and generate revenue.
- Affiliate marketing: You can include affiliate links in your video descriptions and earn a commission on any sales generated through those links.
- YouTube AdSense: As your channel grows and meets YouTube's monetization requirements, you can start earning revenue through ads that appear on your videos.
- Crowdfunding: You can use platforms like Patreon or Kickstarter to receive support from your audience in the form of monthly contributions or one-time donations.

It's important to diversify your revenue streams and not rely on just one source of income. This can help you weather changes in the YouTube algorithm or fluctuations in ad revenue. It's also important to be transparent with your audience about how you're monetizing your channel, so they understand how their support is helping you create more content.

MONETIZING YOUR YOUTUBE CHANNEL

EARN THROUGH YOUTUBE - THE DIFFERENT METHOD

Monetizing your YouTube channel is an important part of making money on the platform.

There are several different ways to monetize your channel, and it is important to understand each one in order to determine the best monetization strategy for your specific channel.

- Ads: Ads are the most common way to monetize a YouTube channel. You can earn money by displaying ads on your videos, and you are paid based on the number of views and clicks your ads receive. YouTube provides a revenue share for ads, meaning you earn a percentage of the revenue generated by ads on your videos.
- Sponsorships: Sponsorships are another way to monetize your YouTube channel. This involves partnering with a brand or company to promote their product or service in exchange for payment. You can also earn money through affiliate marketing, which involves promoting products and earning a commission on any sales generated through your unique affiliate link.
- Merchandise: Many YouTubers sell merchandise, such as t-shirts, hats, and other branded products, as a way to monetize their channel. You can sell your merchandise through your own website, or use platforms such as Teespring or Merch by Amazon to handle the production and shipping of your products.
- Fan Funding: Fan funding, or crowdfunding, is a way to monetize your YouTube channel by allowing your viewers to donate money to support your content. You can use platforms such as Patreon, Ko-fi, or YouTube's Super Chat and Super Stickers to accept donations from your audience.

Overall, understanding the different ways to monetize your YouTube channel is important in order to determine the best strategy for your channel and to maximize your earnings potential.

YOUTUBE'S MONETIZATION POLICIES AND GUIDELINES

YouTube has a set of policies and guidelines for creators who want to monetize their content. The platform provides various monetization options, such as ads, sponsorships, merchandise, and memberships, but there are certain rules that creators must follow to be eligible for monetization. The policies include guidelines on content eligibility, advertiser-friendly content, copyright infringement, and community guidelines.

Creators must ensure that their content follows the community guidelines, which prohibit hate speech, harassment, and other forms of harmful content. Advertiser-friendly content guidelines require that the content is suitable for all advertisers and does not contain any controversial or sensitive topics. Additionally, creators must adhere to copyright laws and only use content that they have permission to use.

To monetize their content, creators must also meet certain eligibility requirements, such as having at least 1,000 subscribers, 4,000 watch hours in the past 12 months, and 10 million Public Shorts View and complying with

YouTube's terms of service and monetization policies. YouTube also has a review process to ensure that creators follow these guidelines and policies.

Understanding these policies and guidelines is essential for creators who want to monetize their content on YouTube. By following these guidelines, creators can ensure that their content is eligible for monetization and can continue to grow their audience and income on the platform.

MAXIMIZE YOUR REVENUE

Maximizing revenue on YouTube requires a well-thought-out strategy that encompasses a variety of monetization options. Advertising is the most common revenue stream for YouTubers. By enabling ads on your videos, you can earn a portion of the revenue generated by those ads.

Another way to generate revenue is through subscriptions, which allow your viewers to pay a monthly fee to access exclusive content, community features, and more.

In addition to these traditional revenue streams, YouTubers can also monetize their audience through other means, such as crowdfunding and merchandise sales. Crowdfunding platforms like Patreon allow fans to support their favourite creators on an ongoing basis, while merchandise sales offer the opportunity to sell branded products like t-shirts, mugs, and other items.

To maximize revenue, it's important to experiment with different monetization strategies and track the results. Test different ad formats, subscription tiers, and merchandise offerings to see what resonates with your audience.

Analyse your metrics and adjust your strategy accordingly to ensure you're making the most of your revenue streams.
It's also important to comply with YouTube's monetization policies and guidelines to ensure that your channel remains in good standing. Violations of these policies can result in demonetization or even account termination, so be sure to review and understand them thoroughly.

Additionally, it's important to be transparent with your audience about how you're monetizing your content to build trust and maintain a positive relationship with your fans.

HOW TO BUILD A BUSINESS AROUND YOUR CHANNEL

SCALE YOUR BUSINESS AND EXPAND YOUR REVENUE STREAMS

S caling your business and expanding your revenue streams means growing your YouTube channel beyond its initial focus and exploring new opportunities to generate income. This can include expanding your content offerings, creating new merchandise or products, launching an online course, or partnering with other brands to create sponsored content.

To successfully scale your business and expand your revenue streams, you need to have a solid understanding of your audience and their needs. Conducting market research and analyzing data from your YouTube analytics can help you identify new areas for growth and revenue.

It's also important to have a clear brand identity and messaging that resonates with your audience, as well as strong relationships with potential partners and sponsors. Building a strong community and engaging with your audience through social media and other channels can help you create loyal fans and attract new viewers to your channel.

Ultimately, scaling your business and expanding your revenue streams on YouTube requires a combination of creativity, strategic thinking, and hard work. But with the right approach, it's possible to build a successful and sustainable business on the platform.

HIRING AND MANAGING A TEAM

As your YouTube channel grows, it may become necessary to hire additional help to manage various aspects of your content creation and marketing strategy. Hiring a team can help you scale your business, take on larger projects, and provide a more consistent level of quality to your audience. Some roles that you may consider hiring for include video editors, graphic designers, social media managers, and business managers.

When it comes to hiring a team, it's important to have a clear understanding of your goals and the roles you need to fill. Develop job descriptions that clearly outline the responsibilities and qualifications required for each position. You can use job boards, LinkedIn, or your own social media channels to advertise your job openings.

Once you have a team in place, it's important to provide clear direction and communicate your vision for your channel. Set goals and expectations for your team members and provide regular feedback to ensure everyone is working towards the same objectives.

Managing a team also involves ensuring that everyone is working efficiently and effectively. Consider using project management tools, such as Trello or Asana, to keep track of tasks and deadlines. You may also need to provide training and professional development opportunities to help your team members grow and improve their skills.

Hiring and managing a team can be a significant investment of time and resources, but it can also provide a valuable return on investment in terms of increased revenue and growth opportunities for your YouTube channel.

PROTECTING YOUR INTELLECTUAL PROPERTY AND
BUILDING YOUR BRAND OUTSIDE OF YOUTUBE

As your YouTube channel grows, it becomes increasingly important to protect your intellectual property and build your brand outside of the platform. One way to do this is by trademarking your channel name, logo, and any other unique identifiers associated with your brand. This will prevent others from using your brand identity without permission and allow you to take legal action if necessary.

Another way to protect your brand is by building a presence on other platforms, such as social media or a personal website. By doing so, you create more opportunities to connect with your audience and promote your brand. It also allows you to diversify your revenue streams and reach new audiences.

It's also important to be aware of any potential copyright infringements when creating your content. Using copyrighted materials without permission can lead to legal issues and harm your brand reputation. Make sure to properly license any third-party content you use, and always give credit where credit is due.

Lastly, it's crucial to monitor your brand's online presence and address any potential issues or negative feedback as soon as possible. Engage with your audience and respond to comments, and be transparent about any changes or updates to your brand. Building a strong and positive brand reputation outside of YouTube can help protect your intellectual property and ensure the long-term success of your business.

BE A YOUTUBER

99 NICHE IDEAS FOR A YOUTUBE CHANNEL

Here are 99 Niche Ideas you could chose for your YouTube Channel:

- Gaming
- Beauty
- Fitness
- Cooking
- Music
- Art
- Technology
- DIY/Crafts
- Travel
- Fashion
- Sports
- Education
- Comedy
- Vlogging
- Product reviews
- Animal care
- Parenting
- Photography
- Business/Entrepreneurship
- Personal finance
- News/Current events
- Mental health
- Science
- History
- Language learning
- Self-improvement
- Nature/outdoors
- Spiritual/Religious
- Cars/Automotive

- Magic/Illusions
- Beauty hacks/tutorials
- Product unboxing
- Gaming reviews
- Food challenges
- Musicals
- Makeup tutorials
- Product comparisons
- Workout routines
- Meditation/Relaxation
- Comedy sketches
- Cooking tutorials
- Music covers
- Art tutorials
- Tech reviews/tutorials
- How-to videos
- Travel vlogs/tips
- Fashion hauls
- Fitness challenges
- Sports news/highlights
- Test prep/study tips
- Stand-up comedy
- Daily vlogs
- Product testing
- Pet training
- Pregnancy/baby care
- Event photography
- Small business tips
- Investment/stock market tips
- Political commentary
- Psychology/Self-help
- Animal documentaries
- Archaeology
- Language exchange
- Life coaching
- Gardening
- Astrology/Tarot readings
- Car maintenance/repair

- Magic tutorials
- Skincare routines
- Gaming walkthroughs
- Recipe challenges
- Musical performances
- Art challenges
- Phone/computer tutorials
- Fashion styling tips
- Fitness motivation
- Sports analysis/predictions
- Homeschooling
- Environmental issues
- Beauty product testing
- Travelogues
- Clothing try-on hauls
- Yoga routines
- Political satire
- History documentaries
- Language lessons
- Personal development
- Nature photography
- Cooking challenges
- Music tutorials
- Art supply reviews
- Gaming tournaments
- Food taste tests
- Musical instrument reviews/tutorials
- Art speed painting
- Coding tutorials
- Travel tips/hacks
- Sustainable living
- DIY home improvement.

98 YOUTUBERS WHO MADE IT

- PewDiePie
- Shane Dawson
- Zoella
- Lilly Singh
- Casey Neistat
- Tyler Oakley
- Jenna Marbles
- Miranda Sings
- Dan and Phil
- NigaHiga
- Michelle Phan
- Rhett and Link
- Grace Helbig
- Smosh
- iJustine
- Ray William Johnson
- Colleen Ballinger
- Philip DeFranco
- Lindsey Stirling
- Dude Perfect
- KSI
- Felix Kjellberg
- Tanya Burr
- Rosanna Pansino
- Tyler Oakley
- Tyler Blevins
- The Slow Mo Guys
- Roman Atwood
- Zoie Burgher
- Epic Meal Time
- Epic Rap Battles of History
- Mr Beast
- Marques Brownlee
- Vsauce
- MyLifeAsEva
- Roman Atwood Vlogs

- TheFineBros
- Lilly Singh Vlogs
- JennaMarblesVlog
- CaseyNeistatVlogs
- Rhett and Link Vlogs
- You Suck At Cooking
- The Game Theorists
- The King of Random
- AsapSCIENCE
- Rosanna Pansino Vlogs
- The LaVigne Life
- Claire Marshall
- Hey Nadine
- Joey Graceffa
- Dan Mace
- Grant Thompson
- Superwoman Vlogs
- Hannah Hart
- ThreadBanger
- Blogilates
- Zoella Vlogs
- Joe Sugg
- Anna Akana
- Sawyer Hartman
- Casey Holmes
- Maddi Bragg
- Andrea Russett
- Ingrid Nilsen
- Zoella Beauty
- Ingrid Nilsen Vlogs
- Connor Franta
- Rosianna Halse Rojas
- Kandee Johnson
- The Ace Family
- RiceGum
- Niki and Gabi
- Bretman Rock
- Safiya Nygaard

- The Gabbie Show
- Jenn Im
- Simply Nailogical
- Laura Lee
- Zoella Lifestyle
- Liza Koshy
- Lele Pons
- Miranda Sings Vlogs
- Miranda Sings Live
- Shay Mitchell
- PewDiePie Vlogs
- Gigi Gorgeous
- Tanya Burr Vlogs
- Laura Lee Vlogs
- FouseyTube
- Emma Chamberlain
- James Charles
- Jenna Marbles Podcast
- Shalom Blac
- Simplynailogical Vlogs
- Rosanna Pansino Live
- Tati Westbrook
- Jeffree Star
- MissRemiAshten

YOUTUBE REWARDS

YouTube offers various rewards and recognition programs to creators who achieve certain milestones or demonstrate exceptional performance on the platform. These rewards not only provide recognition and motivation but also help creators to monetize their channels and grow their audience.

Here are some of the key YouTube rewards and recognition programs:

1.   YouTube Partner Program (YPP): The YPP is the primary monetization program for YouTube creators. It enables creators to earn money from advertising revenue, channel memberships, and merchandise sales. To join the YPP, creators must meet certain eligibility criteria, such as having at least 1,000 subscribers and 4,000 watch hours in the past 12 months, and comply with YouTube's community guidelines and terms of service.

2.   Silver, Gold, and Diamond Play Buttons: These play buttons are awards given to creators who reach certain milestones in terms of subscribers. The Silver Play Button is awarded to creators who reach 100,000 subscribers, the Gold Play Button for 1 million subscribers, and the Diamond Play Button for 10 million subscribers.

3.   Creator Awards: In addition to the Play Buttons, YouTube also offers Creator Awards for creators who reach milestones in terms of watch time. These awards include the Silver, Gold, Diamond, and Custom Creator Awards.

4.   YouTube NextUp: This program is designed to help emerging creators to accelerate their growth on the platform. It provides training, mentorship, and resources to selected creators, who also receive a cash prize and a trip to a YouTube event.

5.   YouTube Spaces: YouTube Spaces are physical locations around the world where creators can access production equipment, studios, and workshops to create high-quality content. Access to YouTube Spaces is free for eligible creators who meet certain criteria, such as having at least 10,000 subscribers.

6.   Super Chat and Super Stickers: Super Chat and Super Stickers are features that allow viewers to purchase and send chat messages and stickers during a live stream. Creators receive a portion of the revenue generated by these features.

Overall, YouTube rewards and recognition programs provide creators with a range of opportunities to monetize their content, grow their audience, and access valuable resources and support.

YOUTUBE PARTNER PROGRAM (YPP)

YouTube Partner Program, which is a program offered by YouTube to content creators to monetize their content and earn money through advertising revenue. To become a part of the YPP, creators must meet certain eligibility requirements, which include having at least 1,000 subscribers and 4,000 watch hours in the past 12 months, as well as following YouTube's community guidelines and terms of service.

Once a creator meets the eligibility requirements and applies for the YPP, their channel is reviewed by YouTube to ensure that it meets the program's policies and guidelines. If approved, the creator gains access to various monetization features, including displaying ads on their videos, receiving Super Chat and Super Stickers during live streams, and offering channel memberships to subscribers.

The YPP also provides creators with access to tools and resources to help them grow their channels and increase their revenue. This includes access to YouTube's Creator Academy, where creators can learn about best practices for creating and promoting their content, and access to a dedicated support team to help with any issues or questions.

It's important to note that being a part of the YPP comes with certain responsibilities, including following YouTube's community guidelines and terms of service, as well as adhering to copyright laws and regulations. Violating these policies can result in a channel being removed from the YPP and losing access to monetization features.

In summary, YPP is a program offered by YouTube to eligible content creators to monetize their content and earn money through advertising revenue, Super Chat and Super Stickers, and channel memberships. It also provides creators with access to tools and resources to help them grow their channels and increase their revenue.

YOUTUBE PLAY BUTTON

There are four types of Playbuttons available to content creators in the YouTube Partner Program (YPP). These include:
1. Silver Play Button: Awarded to channels that reach 100,000 subscribers
2. Gold Play Button: Awarded to channels that reach 1 million subscribers
3. Diamond Play Button: Awarded to channels that reach 10 million subscribers
4. Custom Play Button: Awarded to channels that reach a specific milestone determined by the creator and approved by YouTube (e.g., 50,000 subscribers)

Silver Play Button

The Silver Play Button is a plaque awarded by YouTube to content creators who have surpassed 100,000 subscribers. It is part of the YouTube Creator Rewards program and is considered a milestone achievement for any channel on the platform.

The Silver Play Button features a silver-colored metal frame and a large glass panel in the center that displays the channel's name, along with the YouTube logo and the phrase "Congratulations for surpassing 100,000 subscribers." The frame also has a built-in hanger on the back, making it easy to display on a wall or other flat surface.

The Silver Play Button is a way for YouTube to recognize and reward content creators for their hard work and dedication in growing their channel and engaging with their audience. It is a significant accomplishment for any channel to reach this milestone, as it represents a level of popularity and influence on the platform.

Once a channel has surpassed 100,000 subscribers, YouTube will automatically review the channel's eligibility for the Silver Play Button. If the channel meets the eligibility requirements, YouTube will send the creator an email asking for confirmation of their shipping address. The Silver Play Button typically arrives in the mail several weeks after confirmation.

In addition to the Silver Play Button, the YouTube Creator Rewards program also includes other milestone rewards, including the Gold Play Button for channels that surpass 1 million subscribers, the Diamond Play Button for channels that surpass 10 million subscribers, and the Custom Play Button for channels that surpass 50 million subscribers.

Golden Play Button

The Golden Play Button is a reward that is given to YouTubers who have surpassed 1 million subscribers on their channel. It is one of the most prestigious awards given by YouTube, and it is a symbol of the creator's hard work, dedication, and success.

The Golden Play Button is made of gold-plated metal and has a large, square shape with rounded corners. It features the YouTube logo in the center, along with the creator's channel name and the number of subscribers they have achieved.

To be eligible for the Golden Play Button, a YouTuber must have a minimum of 1 million subscribers and must comply with YouTube's Community Guidelines and Terms of Service. Once a YouTuber reaches this milestone, they can apply for the Golden Play Button by filling out a form on the YouTube Creator Awards website.

Upon approval of the application, YouTube will send the Golden Play Button to the creator's registered address. The award comes in a presentation box and includes a letter from the CEO of YouTube congratulating the creator on their achievement.

Receiving the Golden Play Button is a significant achievement for any YouTuber, as it represents a large and loyal audience that has been built through consistent content creation and engagement. It is not only a symbol of success but also serves as a source of motivation for creators to continue working hard and creating content that their audience loves.

Diamond Play Button

The Diamond Play Button is a recognition given by YouTube to content creators who have surpassed the milestone of 10 million subscribers on their channel. It is the highest tier of play button award available on YouTube.

The Diamond Play Button was first introduced in 2015 and is made of silver-plated metal and features a large diamond-shaped crystal. The crystal is transparent and reflects different colors depending on the angle of light, giving it a unique and eye-catching appearance. The award also comes with a personalized letter from the CEO of YouTube.

To be eligible for the Diamond Play Button, a content creator must have at least 10 million subscribers on their YouTube channel. Once they reach this milestone, they can apply for the award through the YouTube Creator Awards website. YouTube will then review the channel to ensure that it meets the platform's community guidelines and terms of service before sending the award.

Receiving a Diamond Play Button is a significant achievement for any YouTuber, as it represents a massive following and a significant impact on the platform. It also comes with a sense of prestige and recognition within the YouTube community. Many YouTubers who have received this award have proudly displayed it in their videos or on social media as a symbol of their success.

In conclusion, the Diamond Play Button is the most prestigious award that a content creator can receive on YouTube, and it represents a significant milestone in their career.

Custom Play Button

A Custom Play Button is a unique award given by YouTube to creators who have surpassed 50 million subscribers. This award is a one-of-a-kind creation that is personalized for each individual creator. Unlike the Silver, Gold, and Diamond Play Buttons, which have a set design, the Custom Play Button is designed to reflect the style and personality of the creator.

To receive a Custom Play Button, a creator must first reach 50 million subscribers. Once they reach this milestone, YouTube contacts the creator to discuss the design of their Custom Play Button. The creator has the opportunity to work with YouTube's design team to create a unique award that reflects their channel and brand.

The Custom Play Button is made from a variety of materials, including wood, metal, and glass. It often features the creator's logo or branding, as well as their name and the milestone they have achieved. The design can be simple or complex, depending on the creator's preferences.

In addition to being a unique award, the Custom Play Button is also a symbol of the creator's success and influence on YouTube. It is a testament to their hard work, dedication, and creativity, and serves as a source of inspiration for other creators.

Overall, the Custom Play Button is a highly coveted award that represents the pinnacle of success on YouTube. It is a testament to the power of hard work and creativity, and a source of pride for the creators who receive it.

CONCLUSION

SCALING YOUR BUSINESS AND EXPANDING YOUR REVENUE STREAMS

"Passion into Riches: The ultimate guide of YouTube Mastery - The Legacy Edition" is a comprehensive guide for aspiring YouTubers who want to build their brand and earn money through their content.

The book emphasizes the importance of identifying your niche, developing a content strategy, and creating high-quality video content. It also highlights the significance of building your audience through community building, social media, and other channels.

The book also provides insights into the different ways to monetize your YouTube channel, including sponsorships, merchandise, and other revenue streams, and the strategies to maximize your revenue through advertising, subscriptions, and other revenue streams.

In addition, the book covers important topics such as protecting your intellectual property, building your brand outside of YouTube, and hiring and managing a team to support your YouTube channel.

Overall, "Passion into Riches" offers practical tips and strategies for building a successful YouTube channel and monetizing your content, making it a valuable resource for anyone looking to grow their influence and income as a YouTuber.

ABOUT THE AUTHOR

Alphin Joe Plathottam

Hey Sweethearts, Myself Alphin Joe Plathottam, and I am currently in 9th grade. In my free time, I like to pursue my passion for creating tech videos and helping others earn money. My YouTube channel, Bee Happy - Alphin The Tech Explorer, is where I showcase my skills and share my knowledge with the world.

Originally from Kerala, India, I am now residing in Pala. YouTube is both a side hustle and a hobby for me. I am always looking for ways to improve my content and engage with my audience, whether it's through tutorials, reviews, or other types of tech-related videos.

Through my channel, I hope to inspire and educate others who share my passion for technology. I believe that the world is constantly evolving, and keeping up with the latest trends and advancements in technology is crucial. Join me on my journey as I explore the exciting world of tech and share my experiences with you.

In addition to my YouTube journey, I'm also the author of my first book, "Spark of Treasure: Igniting Motivations to achieve your goals." I believe that everyone has the potential to achieve their dreams, and my goal is to inspire and motivate others to pursue their passions and turn them into a successful careers.

www.ingramcontent.com/pod-product-compliance
Lightning Source LLC
LaVergne TN
LVHW060201050326
832903LV00016B/340